# Markers *and* Shrines

Books by Margot Schilpp

*The World's Last Night*
*Laws of My Nature*
*Civil Twilight*
*Afterswarm*
*Markers and Shrines*

# Markers *and* Shrines

Margot Schilpp

Carnegie Mellon University Press
Pittsburgh 2025

Acknowledgments

Many thanks to the editors of the following journals where poems first appeared, often in slightly different versions:

*The Common*: "Acting"
*Diode*: "Inquisition" and "Ode to Moving Targets"
*Failbetter*: "Firsts"
*The Minnesota Review*: "Casualties"
*Stone Highway Review*: "Cry You Mercy"

Book design by Connie Amoroso

Library of Congress Control Number 2025931898
ISBN 978-0-88748-716-3

Printed and bound in the United States of America

10 9 8 7 6 5 4 3 2 1

*for Jeff, Paula, and Leah*
*and for Erich and Joe*

Contents

# Firsts

Imagine the dull lunch hours
at the baking company
in Bridgeport, Connecticut,
where pies and more pies
were turned out for year
after year of Yale students
to eat, then flick their wrists
and let fly the tins, marked
Frisbie Pie Company, until
one afternoon in 1948
someone thought to skip
the pie and get right
to playing the game.
The first plastic Frisbee sold,
then so did a hundred
million more, but a first
is a first. The first cable car
patent in 1871
for the Clay Street Hill Line,
the first motel in the world,
the "Milestone," opened
in 1925 on Highway 101
just north of San Luis Obispo,
the first license plates
(France, 1893).
The Penny Black.
The Gutenberg Bible.
The Morris Worm.
The WebCrawler.
The Tulip Stairs.

Yellowstone's Shoshone
National Forest. We don't
remember what comes next,
but being first at almost
anything assures you
a place in someone's history:
first Microsoft employees,
first call placed on a cell phone,
first Oscar winners,
first image of a tornado, first
casualty of each successive war.

# Archetypes in High Relief

Say you're sitting spread-eagled on a chair, talking
down to the woman on the floor.
Say you are both naked and possessed

by the knowledge that imaginations
tell only one story over and over.
At the restaurant, crayon drawings

repeat: a circle of desire, a square
that keeps you out, spirals
that confuse you and your pets.

I can remember only the vaguest history:
Huns, Babylon, Hittites, formica,
the discovery of the double

helix, Hitler, a membrane of Saran Wrap finally
keeping foods fresh. The ends
of the stories aren't the same:

sometimes the protagonist loses an eye,
or gets the girl, or learns to fly
and gets revenge on every mottled

retriever in the city's crowded pound.
You ordered chocolate cake and intended
to celebrate the loss of every bit

of dignity you ever had. Salud! Bra straps
have slipped into view. Prost! A belch
that would do a professional wrestler

proud escapes from your thin frame.
Cheers! Congratulations, felicitations!
You've shattered a record

for something, even if it's not yet clear
for what. There's half-full for you:
an early celebration and a dizzy focus

on how little we actually suffer.
I've never been good at rituals
and this one's easier than most:

call a friend and ask them to join you
for a drink. It takes a certain kind of atom
whizzing around in anticipation

and a human heart's fragrant chill.
All you see are the smiles positioned
on our faces. All you see is a cordial,

detached seeking. No one says you have
to ring bells or break a piñata.
But a jet with a banner buzzing

behind it would do. Advertise success
and bury failure, even the instructive kind.
You don't want an Edsel full of engineers

roaming I-5 with a shared idea
and the phone number of some call girl
scrawled on a matchbook.

And there's no pleasing you anyway—
not when the guests yell "Surprise!"
and rush forward to say you're gentle

and pretty, you make a mean
boysenberry pie. But now the party's over:
damp cardboard cups and wadded napkins

litter the yard. You'll have to clean up soon
but for now, you'll cross your fingers.
You'll close your eyes.

# Liesl Rehearses on a Quiet Morning

The Captain knocked, hard. He scuffled across
the breakfast nook and his warning stripes
looked out of place at the table. He heard a hunter
in the distance, sneaking up and down the living room
stairs, but the crunch of the flakes was already shifting
to soggy and clawing revenge would have to wait.

He smelled fear in the spoiled milk of his bowl
and in all of Germany there was no more big game
to shoot to the ground. The doorbell played
"The Sound of Music" after years of silence.
And after years of silence it was silent still.

The sink swallowed the whole family's utensils
and everyone wore hand-sewn outfits made
from the ugliest drapes, but the shapes cut out
let the sun in and we tanned until the doomsday clock
struck the world's end. The minor scales of panic
played up our spines. Music couldn't save us.

Memory couldn't prepare us. We met in the gazebo
and danced like a blitzkrieg of rules wasn't strangling
us in our beds every night. But edelweiss was waiting
to be picked in our dreams of climbing and we would
sometimes tear flags in the streets. We hurried
from the stage and fled through black meadows.

The guitar's strings were plucked by no one
and no one heard the notes that hadn't played.
At least that would be what we'd tell the guards

at the border—that our scales fell to clatter
on the villa's marble floors and we would never
again raise our voices nor our children nor our fists.

# Downtown

That summer, it was on the radio every day,
maybe every hour—*When you're alone*
*and life is making you lonely*—but I was two,

so singing along was simply copying sounds:
down-town, down-town, down-down-town,
and then my brother copied me, but

in a lower register, and exaggerating
my slow downs and towns—*dowwnn-towwn*—
adding grimaces for effect, stretching his jaw

wide and then snapping it shut again.
We lived in Chicago then—*Just listen to the music*
*of the traffic in the city*—where trips

to the city's center meant a ride on the El
and some shopping at Marshall Field's.
The winds must have raced between buildings—

*all the noise and the hurry*—, must have chilled
our fingers and noses, and our mother
surely buttoned our coats tight against

grime or shiver. But all that's left to me now
is the refrain and a few verses: *Downtown,*
*Downtown, downtown, some little places to go to*

*Where they never close.* And what's left of
the home we lived in is splinters and ruin:
the new owners leveled it to build

a larger house. One of our neighbors' kids
died of AIDS. An exodus occurred, but slowly,
like a leaking tire. One by one, people moved.

Died. Divorced. *Don't hang around and let*
*your problems surround you, there are movie*
*shows Downtown.* Yet in my mind, the song

plays on a loop. What's far away
comes closer, and *how can you lose?*
*Everything's waiting for you.*

# Cry You Mercy

When the sun slopes into ten,
witches and the chamomile of doubt
brew a strong tea: *drink, my dear, drink.*

You'll see the future in the leaves,
be able to read the truths of layers
and voids, like the inside of a jar

that held something important.
See how the fist holds its secret:
emptiness and nothing more. *It's not pretty,*

*my dear, not pretty.* And you must
remember it all of your days.
Take with you the odd rules: the varied

pronunciations of wound, how to win
an argument, when to give in completely.
These circumstances call for rashness.

This situation calls for the drastic. I see
failures in the eclipse, signs in the artichoke
heart, though what they mean

I can never quite divine, unless it's ordinary
kindness that leaches from within.
You want me to absolve even what you plan

to repeat if you have the chance, and I want
amnesia, oblivion, burial, want every cell
embracing an injurious image or word

to wither and float down the river Lethe.
The art of forgiveness is learned by practice
and necessity—I have known too much of both.

# Imperfect Memory Palace for an Ex Who Died of Early-Onset Alzheimer's

It's only me now.
          I'm the repository
of everything we did
          together and apart.

But we had lost touch.
          I didn't know that for years
now I'd been the only one
          who recalled us. Your memories

leaked away, puddled
          into a bog, never to emerge again.
My prismatic, fragmented images
          of those years will have to do.

*

In the first room, we're in the *New Yorker*'s parking lot
at an evening's beginning. Butch women in white undershirts
and Levi's 501s mix with men flaunting glittery gowns
and expert drag makeup—doppelgängers of Joan Crawford

and Dolly Parton and Barbra Streisand—who glide
toward the red metal door to pay the cover and enter
our town's only gay bar. Disco music carries beyond
the building: "Ring My Bell" and "Bad Girls"

and "We Are Family" blast in heavy rotation. Watery drinks
work for underage drinkers and pot smoke wafts

from the restrooms until we close the bar down, then gather again in the parking lot looking for what's next.

*

Room two is full of water
moccasins flashing

in an abandoned strip pit.
To enter, you need a key

to the gate's padlock.
To leave, you need

the same. We move
through coolers and tents,

sunburns and hangovers,
fireworks shows, card games.

The grass near the water
has thinned to dirt

under the infinite tracks
of our bare feet.

Everyone partying
at the pit has

her topless Polaroid
in the pit owner's album.

*

In room three,
all of my
things are on

fire. You piled
them on the
sidewalk outside our

trailer, then lit
the match. Room
three is ash.

*

In room four there's an aquarium
where gouramis and angelfish
cut through the water and the buzz
of the pump surrounds us.

We sit in front of the glass
and watch the fish follow
one another to nowhere.
They never arrive.

*

Room five's floor is crunchy
with broken glass. Sometimes
when you drink, you shatter things.

Sometimes when you drink
you break up with me. Or you break me.

*

In room six a crumpled motorcycle tank reflects images
from the hospital room where for three months you wear
a pelvic external fixator and hope your fractured pelvis
will mend. Room six is wallpapered with all the flunking
coursework from my second semester in college.
I had not known there were so many ways to fail.

*

Room seven
holds a single piece
of paper:
an AA amends letter
you sent to my mother
more than fifteen years
after we'd broken up.

*

Room eight showers sparks
from a shielded metal
arc welder. You're in training.
You're learning how
to fuse things together.
I pick you up after class,

your off-white overalls
stippled with burn holes.

*

Room nine finds us in a red Gremlin.
You've wrecked your mom's Oldsmobile
and she's had to find a car she can afford.

Before the wreck you'd said: *I've driven
this road a hundred times.* When the car
came to rest halfway down the ravine,

we scrambled away from its carcass across
broken bottles and up the steep hill. I arrive back
where we left the road in one high-heeled Candie's shoe.

*

It's still just me now—me and ash
and muddy ruts in the road to the pit.

Eventually, your mind couldn't hold
long-ago or yesterday, no longer knew

where we went and what we did.
My mind can't quite adapt

to knowing you've tiptoed off
this mortal coil. I focus on finding

in my mind the fragments of days
and hours we spent together—in love,

sampling everything we found
the world offered, or fighting

about the ridiculous and sublime,
but it all disappears like smoke. Like smoke.

# Chaos Theory

A small bump in the galaxy's skin
brought us here: teenage angst
and candy bars, rivets

that work loose and are flung
into the atmosphere,
a general disorder growing

more tangled. The way
to restore a broken thing
is not to break it more.

Mr. Fixit can't always repair
what we bring him. Oh,
he'll try—a badly reconditioned

doll, a vacuum that blows
cosmic dust across the barren plains
of our carpets and floors—

and no one ever tells
him the job was shoddy.
Time is a bookmark

guiding our plans
and we can accommodate
changes and deletions

but there's no corresponding
bang when it comes
to shifting gears. We know

where we want to go.
We know the many ways to get there.

# Stand Up

So long into the black tail of the night,
a pair of headphones covers the power of waves heading into the darkness
to bounce off the stars. I didn't know

anything before the binders allowed me
to read about the guitar. The amp fell off the stage and I meant to pick it up,
but didn't. Stand up means being

on the road that doesn't absorb
light. Laughing is like tenacity. I love words that are funny, or smooth
on the tongue, a lick up the ribs,

a voice that allows my ears to relax.
Then, there's a squeal that comes from under the car's tires. It may be
my imagination. It may be the piglet

that escaped from the field, under
the fence, almost to the road but the girl's arms grab him, pull him
to her chest as she whispers

into his pink triangle ear:
"What's the secret?" The piglet doesn't know the secret, of course, because
a piglet knows mud and sunshine

and sawdust. The piglet knows each moment
as the moment it is. I know that each moment may be the last so the piglet and I
live on different planes. We observe each other

from the plate or oven, a sweet
coincidence in the making. The earthquake of consumption makes subtraction
impossible. There is no way to reduce

what we must have unless the years
ahead provide a calculus of ambition. Dogs and coyotes have natural enemies,
I guess, but what's important is the way

the grass waves when the wind catches it.
Anxieties embrace the discussion we have that suggests there is calm
at some indeterminate point in the future.

I want. I wait. I worry that worry
is damage. I worry that worry is love. There is love in the image that floats
above the door, that flows along

the banks we walk, and the medicine
that we must take is forgetting. The nerves remember, but we don't.
The skin remembers, but I don't

know how skin can cover the walls
or rooms without rending. We can't blow out these candles. They're burning
through the night, through the walls,

through the time of solitude
and diving into the inner song of vision and light. We have a fog that covers us,
makes the difficulty of connecting

into a fractal, the center blooming
into a spiral rose that fights the idea of nothing. There is nothing that nothing
can hold or hear and we have come

too late into the void's void.
It is a centaur, a meadow, a moon, a body, a name, a garden, the center
of thought that pulls and winds.

We remember the days before.
We remember the lines and all our sadnesses. It becomes too much to consider ourselves and we must present

a pass that allows us entry
into the futures of ourselves. There is no way to emerge that will not cause pain.
Turn up the volume.

# Dexterity

The left hand wants
what it wants; the right
to stiff-arm tradition
and the talent
the right hand has
with scissors and rulers.
Yet the left hand can't
do much more than push
a token violet
into the prepared sand.
There's always what
happened and what
happened before what
happened. Sometimes
gauze. Sometimes
a fissure invisible until
you're moving through
it. Sometimes a face
counts once and never
again. It's painstaking
and obvious: loss
becomes a terrible
narrator. The story
can never complete
itself. It stays punctured
like a tin star or
a vaccine scar. It stays
on the same page
year after sad year.

## Collisions

Odd how my two worlds abut one another:
a daughter about to enter her evening shower,

a hot tub in South Carolina where she was probably
conceived. Cleansing is the goal, wasn't the goal,

and these days it's harder for me to remember
or predict what was or will be. Then: there

were so many lies. Now: none that I can think of.
I don't lie anymore because now there's no reason

not to say what's what or who's who. Things are.
The days pass and the nights pass and more days

follow those days and nights. There's a reassuring
regularity to the bills and classes and semesters

and mammograms and report cards and vacations
and all the rest. Nothing interrupts and everything

boils against the backdrop of where I've arrived:
middle age. I possess the drops of wisdom I've earned

by making awful choices. I balance the rising
awareness of death against sunsets and crocuses.

So many choices have led me here: I turned away
from a marriage and toward a future without

romanticism. Every Mother's Day I almost pray,
but instead remember the warped road

I took to get here with the usual breakdowns
and repairs. The sun came out every afternoon.

The water changed whatever was immersed
and no one was left to tell me what to do.

## Since Waves

Since Christmas, since the cutting,
since the medication designed to squelch

the last bits of estrogen roaming
inside me, since regrets,

since wondering,
since never-knowing has been equal

to not-wanting-to-know,
since time immemorial, since when,

sincerely, since it's too late,
since words encumber,

since nothing and no one, since
you've been gone, since I breathe,

since the mist and heavens frown,
since every time I cry, since

nothing can move me more, since
ovens, since smoke, since

rabbits dying, since bees earning
flight, since oars and water, since

mustard seeds planted in bloody soil,
since herbs. Since lies.

# Self-Portrait on the Anniversary of 9/11

I am at the table's head,
nodding mine,
encouraging

students to put words
down on the page

but my screen is snow
is fire is a reckoning.

A blank reckoning.

There is music.
There is silence.
There is the promise
of noise.

Before I know it
I am writing about being laid
under a bush near the public library,

about the wisps
of my parents that return
each fall as I'm starting
the new term,

about climbing the steps
of a clinic in the Haight
and ripping open
a little manila envelope
to scrounge the pills inside.

Or I am imagining that I come
from a bloodline
I could be proud of,
that my reluctance
to seek my birth parents
doesn't stem from fear.

All these days require me
to turn off the news,
to remember that what's in front
of me is what's mine to tend.

I don't need to perseverate.
I can disengage.

I am numb and I am sad.
This combination
means no words escape,

means sometimes I am above
myself, watching
what unfolds,

seeing what can't be seen
at ground level.

From above I can see
a different me, a tentative,
scared imposter.
For a few days rain interferes

with our lives.
Umbrellas and coats
disguise the end of summer.

I tell myself that
there is weather
and there is survival.

# Some Say Fire

The music and the mountains march
down and there's not a lot to think about
now, since everything is ending
in seven years or seventeen,

but either way, we're all finished. No
amount of cajoling or caroling or caressing
will save us now. We're slaloming down, one
hand on the pole and one hand reaching out

to the snow on the trees to catch one
last handful before the planet winks out.
I can't think of how else to say it: we're dying.
Incrementally, sure. Slowly, of course. Happily,

I think, because we no longer have to
make posts or return phone calls or head in
to work when our stupid bosses think
we should be there. We can make decisions.

We can stall and shuffle. We can forget
the dentist and car maintenance. We can leave
those holes in our roofs and our jeans
because now there's no reason to worry.

We're all set and that's that. I've ordered
tens of thousands of dollars of headbands
and slippers and bath soap and marzipan
on Amazon and it all arrives this week.

I didn't order razors. No more shaving!
I didn't order next year's calendar, either.
No appointments! No commitments!
Just the pure sloth of recognizing futility.

And recognize it I do. Is it useless to consider
what's useless? Because how will I know
what to add to my Amazon cart next week?
I surely won't have used up my headbands

and bath soap, but what if everyone is wrong?
I will have severed all my ties to polite society
and for what? For the headiness of hoping
that all the things I do—grading, driving

my daughters around, going to the symphony
with my husband, traveling to see relatives—
all of those things don't now need to happen.
Now I can drink from the milk jug and leave

the Nilla Wafers open. Now I can park wherever
I want and miss doctors' appointments, haircuts.
I can "forget" to answer all emails, and, in fact,
I can skip checking email altogether (unless

there are confirmations about all my arriving orders).
I won't have to shape my eyebrows
or cut my finger- or toenails; I can Howard Hughes
it all day and night. Bring me the Kleenex

and the glass bottles to pee in. Bring me baggy clothes
and curse my friends out as they're rapping
on my door. Skip putting the trash bins out
on Mondays, skip paying those pesky income taxes.

For that matter, let the person who was in charge
of payroll have quit and let my paychecks
keep being direct-deposited forever and ever,
or at least until the final show: the Northern Lights,

which have begun to be seen everywhere,
not just at the highest latitudes.
That's how I want to die—to be struck
by incalculable beauty so hard that it's the end of me.

# A Stranger Speaks of Calamities

There is almost no one's voice I want to hear
who is not already in this house, though
the telephone rings and I answer. A stranger
speaks of calamities. They will befall me
should I not—right now!—go to my computer,

turn it on, turn it over for diagnosis. Bad
programs are already causing the pages I visit
to load slowly, are already reaching for
my bank login and credit card accounts.
I do not fall for this, of course. I have been alive

for more than fifty years. I have sometimes
pretended I am not myself. I have informed
callers I am not at home, but most often, I am
firm and sweet: *Please take me off your list.*
*Goodbye.* Still, I wonder where the callers are

and how they can accept being hung up on
gracelessly call after call, which is how I imagine
most people handle such things. I envision a room
full of men (because it is almost always men
who call about my computer), their backs pin-straight,

their heads down in something like a prayer,
whether that prayer is for release from making
these numbing calls or to reach one soft voice at the end
of the line who'll say, sure, hang on, I'm flipping
the switch now, turning it on. Help me help me help me.

# Acting

The crowds are a loaded pincushion
that pricks me as I lean into
the human tide. The rotunda's marble

smells like forgotten marigolds
left to dry under fluorescent tubes.
Chris Cooper visits the AWP book fair

and for a moment everyone vaporizes—
everyone's body seems to dematerialize—and all
that's left are glossy, artsy covers and a hushed

suspension of subscription spiels.
But my daughters can't be quiet. They want
to tell Mr. Cooper they loved his movie *October Sky*.

They want to explain how much they understand.
They want him to know they know
who *he* is so he'll know who *they* are.

What he wants to know
is whether they liked *The Muppets*
(which they did), and then everyone's bodies

rematerialize exactly where they'd been before.
The trick of time performs itself. We stand
in a hall of dark mirrors staring

at the reflections of other people
where we, ourselves, should be. Then no one
says anything or sees anything. It is a coup

of kindness unfolding. The tables gossip
and chitter in language all their own. They steal
our happiest souls. They regenerate from the tiniest

of roots. The editors dine on despair, and their journals
will swarm toward our houses four times
a year if we promise to act entertained.

# Casualties

The thistle butterflies near the glass collapse
their weight collectively: they

close their wings

*

and it's night again. It's night with a scarlet flash
of light sparking through

the window's bones.

*

It only seems like summer here. Go softly
into the sparse grasses

and ailing trees—

*

sumac, timothy, cocksfoot, oak—the stems
and trunks camouflaging India

ink and eiderdown.

*

Then here again: to be. A simple verb
for a complex state,

all bidden

*

in the aftermath of doubt and crutch and die.
We are, we are: the sudden

crisis undeterred.

*

Be sorry once in a while, even when the jet's
contrails fall to vapor and quit

opposing what has been

*

and then what is. No one can follow you out
of childhood where the butterflies

land, pigments

*

cloaking the wings, the bright cells caustic
to the gray reflections, heavy doses

doubled in the glass.

# Hotlanta

There was a van parked behind the club.
There was music that bled into the night's cool air.

I have considered the scene: leather, sweat, beer, smoke.
I have gone over it in my mind.

Remembering is hard.
Remembering bubbles other memories yoked to these.

Late into the night we swayed.
Late into the night smoke curdled upward.

Lights shine brighter when your eyes haven't yet adjusted.
Lights shine brighter if you're guilty.

No one wanted to tell her how she tripped
across the floor and bumped into people and walls.

No one kept their secrets well enough.

The crowd swelled like a fat lip.
The crowd stood still.

Our table wobbled every time a mug was set on it.
Our table had no vantage point.

We couldn't see ourselves.
We couldn't see three feet in front of us.

Sparrows fell out of the sky.
Sparrows nested in the van's tailpipe.

Their cries were loud in the night.
Their cries made headlines

or maybe that was something else.
Something else made headlines.

Not sparrows. Not lights.
Not beer. Not smoke. Not music.

Not the night's cool air.

# Imaginary Travels

All of the webbing on our old chairs
                        had gone loose. Before the rains,
they would glisten like spider webs.

                        Clearly, it was time to head to Lowe's
or Home Depot or Sears to pick up
                        new teak patio furniture. Driving,

however, was a problem. Every time
                        I got into the car, it rained, and I'd cower
in the driveway, unable to pull into

                        the street. For several years, I'd had kind
neighbors who would drive me where
                        I needed to go. Going anywhere was

complicated. However much I planned,
                        the horses seemed to be out of the barn,
the blackbirds out of the pie. Imperfect

                        as life is, the prospect of rainbows
and unicorns or some other random
                        fairytale feature looms. Justice helps

us understand loss. Kind words open
                        doors that machine guns could spray
with bullets, and even if effervescence

                        bubbles up in the cauldron of greed,
the price for really knowing something
                        is dear. Let me take you beyond words,

beyond sound, to the pasture where
weddings take place while a winter-
coated horse bumps the minister's arm.

He intones the words that will join
these two people, forever, if we're optimists,
to one another in sickness and in health,

with honor and respect, until the born days
disappear up the screen with a little flick
of a finger, and let me remember the way

the meadow smelled, faintly green
with a top note of hope mixed with melancholy
and cheer, until the candles blow out

and turn cold. Mention another's name
and you're sunk. Nevertheless, things move
on, apace. Only a red-winged blackbird

rising from the cattails can save us.
Prevent the future from coming to pass
and you're stuck in the past. Quietly, all

the spooks in Langley go to sleep at once.
Rain sprays the tree bark. Silent moons
circle their planets. Tomorrow is on its

way, but for now, there are errands and chores,
lists that must be completed. Unless you plan
to hightail it out of here one night, you'd better

stock up. Variously, we pack our bags, one
            for every letter in the alphabet. Wait until you
try to pick them up: they're stuffed with all

            the longing we could muster. *X*'s and *o*'s plaster
the sides of every suitcase, remnants of our simpler
            selves. You may not remember yourself then, but

there are snapshots and stubs marking the last
            page you read in each book in the house.
Zip that satchel when you're ready to go.

# Redeployment to the Field of Good Intentions

Why are you all in a dither? The moment
Is the peace you seek, everywhere
And always. Amen. But how

To distinguish love from a heart attack
Or the buzzing of a thousand bees?
You know the answer to every question

Is one more question and an emphatic insistence
On chocolate. Howl if you must: take no
For an answer. It's late in the story

For someone not to die. Let it be the ghost
Of pinking shears that reminds you how lovely
The jagged line can be, that scar

Holding us against our wills.
I am not a guarantee
You'll have storms or sunrises. I resemble

The thickness of a tree. See the branches
Cover the age of immunity. See the waiting
Rooms of doctors' offices and labs.

The fascination of every other milky gaze repeats
The run of pathology. I'm asking you
To shake out the wrinkled shirt

Or the fuzzy logic of attraction; reject the words
You love the most.
The swallows circle in a muddy ellipse, swoop

Down just short of colliding with a rafter.
They look. They fly again.
When the biggest signal is a red noise,

I listen to it fade in, then out.
A note arrives in the mist
Of woe. Each day

The flagstone is silent under the shoes
Of every single settler.
And again I watch the waves mount strategy.

The movement is the movement.
Seek it often, in the darkness, and again.
Rise up, retreat, rise up.

The camera's shutter flags a different scene:
Oyster crackers and swerving flags, half
A pear resting on its round hip.

# Sugar or the Master

Oh, there are so many times I long
            to be sugar or the Master

lock hanging from a hasp,
            but always bells,

always violation against wonder.
            I sort against the tide, prelude

and rhapsody, yet this music
            entices not a thing

but spends its life
            as a blue sun that sets

on the currency of matters
            that don't concern me.

Of the moments I fear,
            the one I am living now

is uncertain mist,
            is braille or blurred,

so that reading
            any small decision

makes me think septic
            think mistake or inevitable

or just damned to repeat
          the cycle of repeating

what hasn't worked before.
          I am loss in flesh.

Don't wander
          away from me now:

I'm talking
          to you. Where are the limits

of what to allow?
          This separateness

works against us
          every time. For love,

there's no excuse, unless you're a painting
          or the deep and bitter moon

shining across the lariat
          of the room's emptiness.

The more I lose,
          the more complete I feel—

people and places lost to me
          inhabit me,

startle me in the dark.
    The self I detest accelerates.

I languish in the sill's afternoon sun.
    I'm so weary of finding

no words.
    Forgive me for my lack

of attention to the things
    large and small,

that would have mattered.
    I am flesh, lost.

The sea lions seduce me—the water
    marks the places I used to be.

All journeys end
    as they begin: bloody

and a fight
    for every breath, for the chords

that wrap themselves into the knot
    that is the noose.

# Toward a Bonfire

The peaches leave slurs on the road,
dark riots of taste fallen from the pits
or smudged into the shoulder, attracting
bees and gawkers and the police cars

with their cherries on: this night is over
for everyone in this car, but there's a final
scene in which the flashback puts
together the skin, unspills the blood

and uncrumples metal. Everyone
smiles and doesn't know any better.
The football arcs under the field lights.
The lights spill into the night's sky.

No one knows how many stars
there really are. It doesn't matter.
They're all there, not here,
so we're willing to trust some best guess.

You could name one as a gift
if you've run out of other ideas,
but you may as well name a piece
of paper or a grain of sand. They're out

there, too, and lonely
among all the other grains and sheets,
among the motes and cells and every
other component of the wholes

we take for granted and hardly see.
The Accord's red paint has flaked
into the roadway where the engine's oil
mixes with the blacktop's film of grease.

The truck was meant to deliver its peaches
to the Piggly Wiggly, but it traveled over
the solid white line, then into the car
headed for the bonfire. We can't see

any reason for most of what happens,
but this spectacular conflagration
is almost a reason or a prayer
that trajectories take us into safety

or danger without regard
for steering wheels or maps or the arc
of the football sailing into the night
over the crowd's heads under the lights

showing us everything that's just
about to happen, without regard for
the crackle of broken chairs
as they're tossed up into the fire.

# Unintended Consequences

Pablo Escobar's hippos roam
and multiply until they escape his villa
and terrorize the nearby towns.
No one thought of what to do

after he was gone or how to contain
these animals no one feeds anymore.
Nor does anyone think of what
it will be like, in the future, to be invisible,

even after having spent a life wanting
to be so, then having that wish
come true so utterly and so shockingly
quickly. I am most often past caring

who looks at me or doesn't
but it wasn't always so. I worried—
constantly, continually, tried
to disappear into the scenery.

If they could worry, Pablo Escobar's hippos
would worry about being caught then moved
away from their halls and courtyards,
away from their rutting against the filigree

railing steering them down the stairs into
the abandoned dining room,
the empty desk and open wound
of property bought on the backs

of dead and dying men. Every year
        a mammogram and every year
                an admonition not to forget
the next time. I was a faithful patient,

presented myself as promised when required.
        I am sure I thought that frequency
                equaled protection. It does not.
I have looked down at the fading incisions

shaped like half-moons, have become a tenant
        of waiting rooms and struck up conversations
                with strangers. I have lain on my back
in rooms full of expensive machines

that whir and measure, that image
        the damage wrought and plot the way out.
                I am alone here but not alone.
As the precise green lines mark the field

of treatment, I hear the nurses leave
        before the rays penetrate my skin,
                my bones. There is no escape but to allow
the damage in. Pablo Escobar's hippos

don't have cancer but I do, or did.
        The cells' replications are out of control
                and as invisible as a species left alone
in a land where it doesn't belong.

At first, we don't notice the kudzu or starlings
flourishing because they fall outside
the expectations of the frame. We see
what we believe we'll see. The hippos

seemed a part of Villa Napolese. The cells
seemed a part of the breast. Youth
seemed a part of me, though I surely knew
it was a temporary occupant.

I am a young woman in an aging body.
On days when my hips hurt I lie down
in the shadow of the future.
On days I don't bleed, I am grateful

those cycles are over. Nights, I pace
the floor. I look for solace
in the harvests of the past.
Some nights disappear behind gauze.

Bandages appear. Smoke escapes.
Small tears in my skin. Abrasions. Bruises
I touch gently then touch again. Some days are silent
and I can't return to them unless I disappear.

I am a young woman in an aging body, and
like Pablo Escobar's hippos, I can walk
unnoticed, unmolested at the edges
of the larger world. Like uncontrolled cells,

I hide in the flesh, in the bone, in plain sight.
            There is a sort of grieving to perform
                        and I don't yet have the hang of it.
I look down and am surprised, again.

# We Disappear

Poof! Every human being on earth
disappears at once. We're dust to be swept
from the kitchen floor, but there's no one
to hold the brooms. Or we're ash to be scooped
from the fireplace, but there are no hands
left to hold the shovels. No mail is delivered
to no one. No cars are driven from the spots
they stopped when people vanished. Cougars
and Camrys and Explorers and Impalas idle,
then die, on every road and path. Ox-carts
are unsteered. Bicycles rest at uneasy angles.
The lights, at first, continue to burn,
then fewer do, then none. Donuts harden
on their plastic trays and many buttons go
unpushed. Entropy is quicker with nothing
in its way: sills rot, roofs leak, trees and weeds
seek space and light. Fido and Fluffy go feral
without regular kibble and bites of fish.
Cash drawers gleam with change unspent.
No engines drone, no children squeal.
Nothing interrupts the sound of nothing
moving or crying or smartly falling down.
Sweaters lay flat in flat drawers
while toilets go unflushed. Weeds spread
the macadam into independent continents.
Our buildings lose boards and brick to time,
and time loses sense to an abyss
The world repairs itself. We're not watching
everything grow over, but it does.
No checks are cashed and windows aren't

looked through. Boats arrange themselves
back into planks, harps return to string
and frame, books go unread and music unheard.

# The Parties

From the trunk of the car to the liquor cabinet,
it's fifty-four steps, give or take. With a box in hand,
it's a long trip. Gin goes here. Scotch there. Vodka

and mixers here. The shiny, round penguin ice bucket
reflects bottles and the door's louvres, the cardboard
box with separators balanced on the dining table.

This evening, I balance on my father's lap watching
for the sweeping of cars' lights in our driveway.
He peeks at his watch: time for the guests to arrive.

For me, it's time to help arrange the cheese platter
and the slices of ham, smile when the bell rings
and the door opens on one more couple

or old friend who's spending the evening perched
on the couch, cowering away from our vicious cat.
More than one guest leaves with a Band-Aid across

punctured skin. I always feel like furniture
being shown off—see the finely turned legs,
the shiny, wavy hair. Everything centers

on surfaces: on how we look instead
of how we feel about all those conversations,
all those slow hugs, all those early mornings

of vacuuming and dusting and straightening
the rooms that hours later will be the stage.
My favorite part of every evening is the collapse

of the air back into itself after the last guest
has left and the cleanup work begins.
Even the cat retreats from her exhaustive vigilance.

# Simplify

Often I imagined simplicity as the center
of a vast well of dark fear that radiated
out, something to be summoned

infinitely, indefinitely. Skirts and wagons
and spokes were turning up and turning around
while depth soundings and the business

of sugar plantations ebbed far into
past tense. Overridden debt claimed
the homestead and the last things made: false

teeth with a surname miniaturized into the gum
so as not to be lost at the nursing home's
mass bathings. Or I noticed it among

the daffodils and peonies that came back
every spring, or in the rusty hasp of the shed's lock
which refused to open on humid days.

Inside was the hand-tooled bridle, the masculine
flowers rubbed into the leather in a pantomime
of beauty. Often I wandered back

to that field where the horses stood in the clover
and I sat down in the mounds of grass
that encroached on the city limits.

I wanted to listen to Mrs. Kelly's genteel drawl
while I sat on her porch and watched the cars
pass and raise dust. I wanted to follow her

example of smoking and rocking.
That motion saves me:
I rock in the saddle when I ride across

the road. The black rock trail
meanders over acres of woods
where I can guide my horse through mud

or across little streams to cool his hooves.
Sometimes the simplest thing
is the one you can't repeat. I can't go back

to that place. That time is gone, that spot
now cultivated for genetically modified corn
experiments by Monsanto. I would go there,

though, no matter how far the drive, no matter
how different the place. Another simple thing
that can't be repeated: family. They're dead

or scattered to the wind's currents. Most
of the time I can get by without recognizing
that my mother and father are dead,

but sometimes reality comes crashing
the party: they are not here. They are not
anywhere. Simple.

There were brown spots cut off, ointments
salved into the skin, the indignity
of the catheters, the dribbling across the pile.

There was a clock with half a face, the hands
drawn into tight fists, applesauce rush
down the chin. That time shimmers.

Now, when I think of my family,
it is the bland facts I recall—not the dramatic.
Not the sheer astonishment of all of us

improbably fitting together, but each
as the individual, the cog, the tackle,
the gear, the part. My mother used to ask

why I never wrote happy poems.
I thought I had been. I was happy
writing poems. And I have tried

to reconstruct other circles,
the names of each guest perched
on a gray folding chair: Ron, Carl, Wendy,

Leslie, Oliver, Kim. Their voices pierce
time, bounce off the silver coffee urn
and get buried in the shag. I try

to listen to the old complaints but the future
intrudes: now, now, now, do, do, do.
Don't go back and marry the class clown. Don't

speed on old Route 13 the night a deer
lopes across your lane. Don't pretend
the car was stolen when your father notices

it missing from the driveway. Don't arc
off the rocks into a nest
of copperheads roiling under the dark water.

# Re-photographs

Inside us somewhere must be
a mislabeled organ
or gland that we think regulates

thyroid hormone or sexual desire,
but that really tells us to go back
to try to decipher what's gone wrong,

patch the crumbled tuck-pointing
of a twenty-year friendship.
Some people photograph their kids

in the same pose at the same place
year after year to document
time's cheery disregard

for itself, though in re-photographs
out in nature, the largest boulders
or scrim of landscape arrest

what doesn't change. But what varies
endures too: unmoving trees, a display
case built into the side of a building,

a blur across the lens. We look and want
to look again. What has changed
and what remains? Notice the sky,

with its decades-old clouds,
bumping up against the photo's edge.
Notice the 1906 Ramblers nosing down

Market to survey the smoke and cracks,
or panzer tanks capturing the streets
like uncouth boys in a china shop.

And notice the calm growth
of ivy up the stadium's walls. Don't
scrimp on description or detail, for

it is the same brick of a window box,
or the recognizable shape of a fountain
or road or mount of land that travels

from 1945 Dresden or 1999 Izmit
into photos of those same places now
that lets us see how far destruction

goes toward cobbling everything
together, blurring the distinctions
we want to make between present

and past, right and wrong, alive
and dead, the vanished, the pathetic,
the true and the almost true.

# Ode to Moving Targets

He drinks milk when it's offered. He sleeps enclosed
by wood. The couch and stairs and water are not yet those

things. They are blur and want-to-touch. He always thought the way
stars know us was wrong and that raccoon always scurried

onto someone else's roof, but this morning the bees draw
his attention. They buzz and you buzz. He sees

the handsome beads of jade, a cup on a counter edge,
a quarter coming to rest after spinning. He sees a monument

or hands that reach deep into the future's neck
to pull out vein and cord. Sixty years ago sparrows built

under this bridge, their muddy nests clinging to the timbers.
The bellows of wings pried open the wind and in the stagnant

water below, a blur of brown baskets. A reflection can never be
precise enough to make decisions by: one whorl transferring

energy from the center throws the whole thing out of whack,
but we depend on likeness all the same. If there is certainty

in the chambered nautilus or the armadillo, it's lost
to constant renderings. Believe the outlines you can feel,

the margins that slip against the fingertips, not the signs
that vanish when you choose to close your eyes.

It's like imagining disease: coal dust settles densely
in a young man's lungs, time-bombs, disruptions

marking him invisibly from the inside, corrosion starting
from the center out, so that only more injury can reveal

that damage has already been done. His job now is to stand
utterly still, absorb shock, and pretend

he might catch up with decay's head start. He's been drinking
the milk. He's been sleeping. He is already dying meat.

# On Belligerence

Be contrary. Decide not to
go along with the plans.
Better to think *yes* but shake my head
from side to side, enchant them
with a scowled refusal.
I'm mean, and they know it.
Whenever a ghost of assent prickles
up my spine, I squash it, a harmless spider.
If too early the gums and crowns reveal
themselves behind my lips. I squelch
the smile and rocket straight to *can't*.
There's something salvageable
in crankiness, as long as no one drowns.
The water's deep, but clear: fall
into every hole you can. Have a costume
for opening the door. Be invisible
and silent in the meetings
you attend. The oceans ebb
and flow. So can my commitments.
All the common latitudes we cross
began as chips on someone's shoulder.
I've learned how to refuse
in the meanest possible way.
Children take me at my word
especially when it's *no*.

# Lines Composed of Fragments of Twenty Student Essays

A story that discussed heritage,     the importance
    of togetherness,     a desire to belong within
a group—     all of these help to connect
    the blind man's wife dying     and a loving
personality,     a selfish lover, and     the ability
  to focus on friendship.   It can be faked
    for some people,     but assigned in infinite ways.
If I cannot trust them,     there are nerves
and migraines     and money worries,     victims
    of treachery.     Who is socially awkward?     The city,
his mother in a rocker,     their significant other.
    The first way is love,     a slight problem,
their separate ways.     He is willing     to ruin
    their marriage,     to fight for the wife,     to visit,
to love her more than anything.     A mother
    has gone crazy.     When they are good
they have the strongest bond, though others
    are vastly different     in our society today.
Many stories throughout time     do not have children
    or a smile.   Motherhood is a metaphor
and an experience,   a point of view,     a concept
in the past while     snippets tell something
    of the three.     All that really matters   in the world
is two themes     that help us get the most
    out of life.     Not everyone is perfect,
and she was a single     teen mom,     a daughter,
first born,     taken for granted,     swallowed
    by greed,     no miracle at all.     All of her
baby loveliness had gone,     and what he saw
on paper,     already looked     ironically the same.

# Inquisition

They asked her about geometry
and she replied with a description
of the discovery of penicillin. They asked
her about the guillotine and she told them
about beignets and baba au rhum.
They asked her about phobias. She told
them about religion, about love
that happens offstage. They asked
her about Galileo, and she mended
the hems of their maps. They inquired
how to make a fortune and she alluded
to Darwin. They wondered when
the earth began and she clicked
her stopwatch, her heels, her pen.
They asked why we made streets
and she took off her shoe. They asked
her about etiquette and she gave a lecture
on the constellations. They wondered
why photographs feel so believable
and she bought them tickets
to Spain. They asked about
exposition. She handed them puppets.

# In Case of No Itinerary

I have the miser's touch,
the monkish silence
on the other end
of the phone.

What counts as vanity
among the sparse,
brown grass? It can be
the mirror, sleeping.

What hackles
of dense claw and spangle dart
from underneath the trees?
There is dilation

and metaphor on the wind.
I want to see,
but everything is opaque:
blur, blur, the Gaussian

cover and details,
blunted into a nicer version.
A month of drought,
a red hammock

dotted from the rains.
I find the scent
of a circle. Sunlight
peels back the blindness

of desire.
I tried candor,
but it was all
lost. Now, look

at the changing: it was flesh,
it was an egg,
it was a scab or a date
made in the heat. See?

One foot,
then the other, on
the next stone.
There is a temple

of birds, a tree
sending sap along
the barky rivers that all flow
down. The layers.

Then, round: a pregnant
belly near due,
a library book on the hall table.
The sticky clear

dented drops and
their reflection of
the reflection of
the perfect sky, inverted.

# Commerce

I wanted a skein of violet yarn,
but the dye lots were mixed,
so when the box arrived, I found

a bright red, and maybe the woman
who packed my order gasped
at the blood color, her high school

sweetheart's car arriving—cherry
red—at her door even after her father
had said she couldn't ride

in convertibles, not tonight,
not ever and the sad-faced boy moped
back out to the street and sat

on his crimson seats, turned the key
and drove out of her life. Maybe
what flashed across her mind

was a scarlet tanager winging
across the electric sky, or fireworks
in July, or the flushed skin

of a fresh apple ready to pluck
from the orchard's oldest tree.
I want to know how quickly

she glanced at the mixed-up numerals,
and whether a field exists where
mistakes float for a moment

before they settle into being
mistakes, a ripple-time when—
before it's over—one could prevent

error from settling around our feet
like broken glass. The cherries
by the roadside, packed

into a corrugated box flash
as I drive by. The hummingbird's
feeder sways when the nectar's sipped,

when flight causes the ripple to move
the tube, and the wind carries
the color of rubies up, across the branches,

maybe to the very tree
that will be felled to make the box
my yarn arrives in.

# Elderly Neighbor, Three Houses Down

First, there are misunderstandings, luncheon dates
when she shows up at the wrong restaurant,

or believes she has money with her, yet all
she can extract from her handbag is fuzzed tissue

and a program from *Hamlet* performed two years ago.
My mother and she, both widows, make plans

to attend a concert, but she steps out of her car
in a
          soiled housedress. Instead,
                                                            they build a fire
and sip cocoa late
          into the evening.          A year or so later,
her only living daughter flies
          twelve hundred miles          every two weeks,
                              then rents a car
to drive a hundred more
so together
                    they can sort out the house
while she still remembers
                                                  which things
she loves.
She spends hours
in her garden,
planting and replanting
riots of marigolds,
zinnias, geraniums, pinks,
her fine,

white hair
in a
comb, caught
like
a vowel
in
her
throat.

# Atlas of Ruin

There is nothing else to do so I listen
for the thought of rain: it comes
without wetness,
                in the morning's gray,
under the shades and across
the room's lifting night fog. It sounds
ancient and angry, full
of threats—
    *your crops will fail*
and *Las Vegas will go dry*—though surely
what is said is not what's meant.
I believe that often—and sometimes
when I speak with you—
                                and the rain
reminds me that there's hope
after a night of churning the sheets
and trying to corral my thoughts
into obedient horses,
        into slippers
of glass, into projections that are like
metaphors are to something real: better
at saying what we really meant.
And just as the phantom rain dots
the sidewalk, the street, windshields,
trees—all the anchors
        of my journeys—
I am going somewhere soon and I travel
farthest in the dark: I travel across the continent
to you.
   Some summer day, years from now,

I want to watch the tide release itself,
remember how I invented happiness
out of a single match, a baseball glove,
the elegant ruins
    of masonry and wood.
So say it with me now: there
will be light and water and time
enough to pledge one and another into
the metronome's dark wing,
into rising
dough, into orange bliss at the end of a fuse.
I'll hold the rocket in my hand.

# Ravel

See the old woman? Her aversion
to ridding herself of her things brought me
a '40s-style jacket—two huge black buttons

on the front and a gorgeous cut that made me feel
famous. She lasted until August of 1982.
She never cleaned out the rooms

in her house, left them to the mildew
and her grandniece sotted under the hot spell
of gin. There in the end-of-summer heat,

shovels full of rotted fabrics, damp piles
of crumbling papers, crusted dishes and mugs
and silverware emptied fifty years into one

brick-red dumpster sinking from its weight
into the street's asphalt. Years later,
my mother's final illness, and for a few weeks,

I was unaware that she was going to die,
thought the nurses' attempts at rehab,
and the heavy oomphs she'd spill

at simply sitting up in bed would fade
and we'd again enjoy lunch at Hunan
or a quick trip to the mall to check out shoes.

I was a thread tying my past into some sort
of future, but the raveling had begun
with her half-faced clock drawn

on a stenographer's pad. She was slipping
into the past tense, and though she gave
a little tug here or there, she was tied

to nothing then. I wanted to untangle the story,
but my grip on things was too solid
to understand how one might be required

to let the story go. It is an accident
and a decision. The nurses came and went.
They straightened the room. I slept

in shifts and worked in the fluorescent bowl
of the hospital's room, certain the brief ordeal
would be ending. And it did end,

thirteen days into the last month
of the 20th century. We'd collected
a lot of props to line the window's ledge.

We'd pulled the privacy curtain to talk
in quiet voices of disbelief and shame.
In the other house, I'd found

a calendar from 1941, austere marks
in an austere time. The salvage operations
continued through rooms and piles.

The fixtures, removed. The last time
closing the door. Another end.
From there, the black jacket hung

for many months, unworn and shapeless.
On the final day of my mother's life
I sat listening to her breathe

through a green mask, a ghosty wheeze
turned both regular and strange.
After her last breath, the nurse came

to arrange her, to help me see her one last time.
I walked back in too soon, caught him
pulling her heavy arm over

the stark white sheet, then over
the massive wound in her abdomen
that they had never closed. It was held

together with two stainless staples
that pulled her skin together
like a too-tight jacket, as though

it could keep her warm and hold
her guts in place. He tried to throw
the sheet over her, but I had seen

and could never stop seeing.
She would have been appalled.
Heads would have rolled.

# Sixty

From the room's threshold I see ambulance lights
disappear around a corner while the siren

moves farther away and I know they're not
there for me, but maybe for someone I love—

my husband or daughters—or a neighbor or
my brother who's been in this room a while.

He told me nothing. No one did. It's all
a mystery, apparently, what is coming toward

us, until it arrives and we are swept into
the corners to bide our time until it's time.

It's time to reassess. It's time to let go
of many good things I've been saving

for someday. Someday is here. I can use
all the china, the stemware, the cashmere,

the fanciest tablecloth, the long-treasured
objects stowed carefully under cabinets

and in closets, draped in plastic to protect
the pristine. I have spent decades not

using things, tucking them away for
some perfect future where I live a life

that's nothing like this one. The cabinets
surround all that promise and hide it

from view. When I decide to leave I will
be decked out in the glamour I kept

from me for years and years. I will drag
my shearling coat across the gravel

and asphalt. I will walk out of this room in style.
Over my shoulder, I will snap a photo I'll leave behind.

# Faux Princess Looks Askance

She is practicing the sidelong glance,
the look that tells a stranger story
than ten little tomato plants all

in a row, a rowboat tethered
to the yellow moon. She is growing
up fairly real, with tea sets and cars

that do what things do in the kitchen
and road, politeness learned
by pretending to care about mealtimes

and distance and hiccups and size,
the shorthand for boys, the dances
of pairs of rodents who pull

the carriage along to the ball
that's occurring this evening among
the glitter of eyes that see surface

as every bit as crucial as her liver
or kidney, the pigments of process
that filter, that bring things

into balance despite a true count
of doughnuts and coffees,
cheesecake consumed in the back

of a truck with her best friend's
groom. He's dressed in a tux,
and though he's shed his shoes

his wallet's intact and wondrously
over the top of the tents
there's a sudden dove-rise.

White moves. By the thousands, wings
stir a great breeze that cools down
cheeks and seals the reunion

of child and farce. All the guests'
faces lift, too. They track
the greenery, the cameras, the rice

diffusing into smoke that forms
dainty puffs. They take wing
against everyone's will.

# Living Arrangements

Nights were loud in that house with its cedar and glass,
confinements beautiful and absorbing, like color

collecting light until it's saturated and has to give
something back. Brightness the shade of hay drifts in.

Crickets strategize. There must be a plan to all this
disorder, a reason that the lines miss connecting

and the scarlet curtains praise the fading qualities
of the sun. Years unrolled like a tape measure, calculating

precise geometries of anger, the angles of slammed doors,
the exact number of minutes it takes a pork chop

to cool. Longer than Cronkite's half-hour drone about the moon
landing or gas lines, and longer than any discussion of divorce.

Some words pierce the walls. They're mosquitoes buzzing
around an ear. They're swatted away to silence, lapping

the long hall. How long can she simmer there in her room,
blaring music and plucking eyebrows into scythes?

# Lullaby with One Party Missing

The stutter of wings maddens
the air there. Come tell me again.

The cradle has rocked, double
time: again grease goes dirty

into drains and heads toward
a miracle, the ticking hour saying

Goodbye all that, goodbye.
It's June, month of fathers.

Mine has taken his books
into heaven. I can't make

the vibration that would let me
tell him everything's fine here.

At the end, I said farewell
and mixed a formula for grief. The pattern

did not hold; it was all wave
and crest. Simultaneity. I needed

proof and then there were poppies
blowing everywhere, their red

regret holding onto the soil's
forgiveness. If only the rules

were beautiful notes.
But some music reaches only

the patient. Some music is eccentric
and false to every ear. The hasp

of time holds fast: he will
not sing me down again.

# Modern Architecture

—for L. P.

Here is a breadcrumb trail of brick
columns, atop which are lights casting haloes
to the ground, and into those haloes pass

students twitchy to get to the next class,
their "real" lives, the library, or the car,
and the bricks that make up the columns

come from somewhere and the sod
they pass by comes from somewhere else,
and the baseball cap canted on a head

from still another place, all of which are not
here, and maybe not in a radius of fifty miles
from here, but the columns stay in their places

and the students keep passing them without thought,
oblivious to the engineering and knowledge
it takes to plan a campus and wire the fixtures

and propose spots that may lure a restless
kid to sit for a while and think about
the impermanence of bodies and the semi-

permanence of structures, for after a while
the columns will crumble a bit and a bit more
and the students will pass from one roster

to others, then finally on. A semicircle
of variegated chrysanthemums blooming now
is the mulch of tomorrow. The stunning

orange leaves trembling to the asphalt become
the rot of the years that christens us with gravity,
and even while we scarcely notice the leaves' falling

and the columns collapsing—which we won't equate
with anything, least of all with our painful knees
or backs, or that one gray hair that we pluck and let fly

into the wind—the first lines of a new design sit lightly
on the drafting table in front of a student aching
to honor someone's early, early death. She hadn't

yet thought of the world as a dying place,
as an abattoir, as a drying hook, as the rock
where carrion is spread to dry.

# Surprise!

A hundred times, a thousand times,
	we've told you not to
jump out from behind or beneath
	to thrill to the faces you see
when we're startled, again,
	by the huge grin and the small word—

*Surprise!*—that seem to get us
	every time. How many
times have I thought *So this is*
	*what my parents, our parents,*
*must have endured, so*
	*this is how they must have felt,*

as we repeat the admonition "don't" in voices
	we understand emerge
from the curtain of years long fallen
	across a decaying stage.
Every time it feels new to you.
	It's clear you haven't listened,

haven't learned what we patiently
	(and not so patiently) explain.
One day something else
	will fascinate you enough to perform it
over and over, *don't* or no,
	or one day we'll grow to expect

the sharp rise of your head into
	our fields of vision as you thrill to the word

again: surprise! I'm here
            and you didn't expect it, did you?
One day, we'll bow and give
            a small wave to the last audience, turn

and exit behind the heavy drapes.
            One day: we're here, then we're not, and though
we all know the ending, it's still
            enough of a shock to draw the coveted gasp,
make us step sharply back,
            cry out loud. Surprise.

Previous titles in the Carnegie Mellon Poetry Series

2012

*Now Make an Altar,* Amy Beeder
*Still Some Cake,* James Cummins
*Comet Scar,* James Harms
*Early Creatures, Native Gods,* K. A. Hays
*That Was Oasis,* Michael McFee
*Blue Rust,* Joseph Millar
*Spitshine,* Anne Marie Rooney
*Civil Twilight,* Margot Schilpp

2013

*Oregon,* Henry Carlile
*Selvage,* Donna Johnson
*At the Autopsy of Vaslav Nijinksy,* Bridget Lowe
*Silvertone,* Dzvinia Orlowsky
*Fibonacci Batman: New & Selected Poems (1991–2011),* Maureen Seaton
*When We Were Cherished,* Eve Shelnutt
*The Fortunate Era,* Arthur Smith
*Birds of the Air,* David Yezzi

2014

*Night Bus to the Afterlife,* Peter Cooley
*Alexandria,* Jasmine Bailey
*Dear Gravity,* Gregory Djanikian
*Pretenders,* Jeff Friedman
*How I Went Red,* Maggie Glover
*All That Might Be Done,* Samuel Green
*Man,* Ricardo Pau-Llosa
*The Wingless,* Cecilia Llompart

2015

*The Octopus Game,* Nicky Beer
*The Voices,* Michael Dennis Browne
*Domestic Garden,* John Hoppenthaler
*We Mammals in Hospitable Times,* Jynne Dilling Martin
*And His Orchestra,* Benjamin Paloff
*Know Thyself,* Joyce Peseroff
*cadabra,* Dan Rosenberg
*The Long Haul,* Vern Rutsala
*Bartram's Garden,* Eleanor Stanford

2016

*Something Sinister,* Hayan Charara
*The Spokes of Venus,* Rebecca Morgan Frank
*Adult Swim,* Heather Hartley
*Swastika into Lotus,* Richard Katrovas
*The Nomenclature of Small Things,* Lynn Pedersen
*Hundred-Year Wave,* Rachel Richardson
*Where Are We in This Story,* Sarah Rosenblatt
*Inside Job,* John Skoyles
*Suddenly It's Evening: Selected Poems,* John Skoyles

2017

*Disappeared,* Jasmine V. Bailey
*Custody of the Eyes,* Kimberly Burwick
*Dream of the Gone-From City,* Barbara Edelman
*Sometimes We're All Living in a Foreign Country,* Rebecca Morgan Frank
*Rowing with Wings,* James Harms
*Windthrow,* K. A. Hays
*We Were Once Here,* Michael McFee

*Kingdom*, Joseph Millar
*The Histories*, Jason Whitmarsh

2018
*World Without Finishing*, Peter Cooley
*May Is an Island*, Jonathan Johnson
*The End of Spectacle*, Virginia Konchan
*Big Windows*, Lauren Moseley
*Bad Harvest*, Dzvinia Orlowsky
*The Turning*, Ricardo Pau-Llosa
*Immortal Village*, Kathryn Rhett
*No Beautiful*, Anne Marie Rooney
*Last City*, Brian Sneeden
*Imaginal Marriage*, Eleanor Stanford
*Black Sea*, David Yezzi

2019
*The Complaints*, W. S. Di Piero
*Brightword*, Kimberly Burwick
*Ordinary Chaos*, Kimberly Kruge
*Blue Flame*, Emily Pettit
*Afterswarm*, Margot Schilpp

2020
*Build Me a Boat: Words for Music 1968–2018*, Michael Dennis Browne
*Sojourners of the In-Between*, Gregory Djanikian
*The Marksman*, Jeff Friedman
*Disturbing the Light*, Samuel Green
*Any God Will Do*, Virginia Konchan
*My Second Work*, Bridget Lowe

*Flourish*, Dora Malech
*Petition*, Joyce Peseroff
*Take Nothing*, Deborah Pope

2021
*The One Certain Thing*, Peter Cooley
*The Knives We Need*, Nava EtShalom
*Oh You Robot Saints!*, Rebecca Morgan Frank
*Dark Harvest: New & Selected Poems, 2001–2020*, Joseph Millar
*Glorious Veils of Diane*, Rainie Oet
*Yes and No*, John Skoyles

2022
*Out Beyond the Land*, Kimberly Burwick
*All the Hanging Wrenches*, Barbara Edelman
*Anthropocene Lullaby*, K. A. Hays
*The Woman with a Cat on Her Shoulder*, Richard Katrovas
*Bel Canto*, Virginia Konchan
*There's Something They're Not Telling Us*, Kimberly Kruge
*A Long Time to Be Gone*, Michael McFee
*Bassinet*, Dan Rosenberg

2023
*Night Wing over Metropolitan Area*, John Hoppenthaler
*Phone Ringing in a Dark House*, Rolly Kent
*Fleeing Actium*, Ricardo Pau-Llosa
*Approximate Body*, Danielle Pieratti
*Wild Liar*, Deborah Pope
*Joy Ride*, Ron Slate

*That Other Life,* Joyce Sutphen
*Sonnets with Two Torches and One Cliff,* Robert Thomas

2024
*Accounting for the Dark,* Peter Cooley
*Shine,* Joseph Millar
*Those Absences Now Closest,* Dzvinia Orlowsky
*Blue Yodel,* Eleanor Stanford
*Her Breath on the Window,* Karenmaria Subach
*Museum of the Soon to Depart,* Andy Young

2025
*Just About Anything: New and Selected Poems,* Jonathan Aaron
*The End of the Clockwork Universe,* Fleda Brown
*Goat-Footed Gods,* Kathleen Driskell
*Pine,* Jonathan Johnson
*Requiem,* Virginia Konchan
*Angel Sharpening Its Beak,* Michael McGriff
*Trying x Trying,* Dora Malech
*Markers and Shrines,* Margot Schilpp